THE HANDSTAND

by

Barry Rudner

Illustrated by Peggy Trabalka

ISBN 0-925928-05-4

Printed/Published in the U.S.A. by Art-Print &
Publishing Company. Tiny Thought Press is a trademark
and service mark of Art-Print & Publishing Company.
Publisher is located in Louisville, Kentucky
@ 1427 South Jackson St. (502) 637-6870 or
outside Kentucky 1-800-456-3208

Library of Congress Catalog Card Number: 90-84065

To Aaron
I shall forever honor
the ground you wheel on.

There once was a club that met after school, to belong to this club there was only one rule.

1

It wasn't
a password
or learning
commands.
You just had
to learn
to stand on
your hands.

To some
this was easy,
or nothing
at all.
Although
upside down,
they all
stood up tall.

For one
little boy
with all of
his might
as hard as
he tried
it never
was right.

He tried
against walls.
His friends
lent a hand.
He just could
not learn
to stand on
his hands.

He practiced
from morning.
The boy tried
through dinner.
The contest
was here
to pick the
big winner.

5

The child
to hold
the handstand
the longest
was known
in the club
as the strongest
of strongest.

He watched
from a distance.
The boy
felt alone.
But another
was watching
from a steel,
wheeled throne.

The boy
walked away
scuffing
his heels,
he noticed
this child
in the seat with
four wheels.

This girl in
the chair
then said
with a grin,
"I know of
a way
you surely
can win."

"How?" asked
the boy
who could
walk on
two feet.

"Simple."
she answered,
as she sat
in her seat.

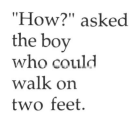
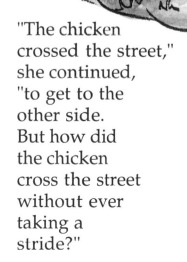

"The chicken
crossed the street,"
she continued,
"to get to the
other side.
But how did
the chicken
cross the street
without ever
taking a
stride?"

9

The boy who
could walk
then scratched
his head,
unsure what
the girl
in the seat
had said.

In the back
of his mind,
the boy
truly knew,
the contest
was near.
He had not
a clue.

He picked
up a stick
and began
to fiddle.
He spelled
the word
"HANDSTAND"
as he pondered
the riddle.

All of
a sudden,
the boy
looked
to see
that he
had forgot
to cross
the T.

"That's how
the chicken
crossed
the street,"
he said,
"without
moving
its feet!"
He skipped and
cart-wheeled
around his friend,
the girl who
lived in the seat.

13

"Come on"
he said,
"before
they begin.
You taught
me the way
that we both
can win."

They wheeled
and walked
as fast as
they could.
They joined
the line
where the
members
all stood.

The members
just laughed.
They did not
understand
how the boy
and his friend
could do a
handstand.

But when it was time to start their handstands both lifted their feet and stood on their hands.

17

One by one
as they rolled
to the ground,
the members
could not
believe
what they
found.

And when the
two friends
were the
last two
to beat,
the boy who
could walk
rose first
to his feet.

This boy who
could only
think about
winning,
thanked his
friend who
sat there
just grinning.

The boy
who could
walk then
turned to
the crowd.
He quietly
said in a
voice true
and proud.

"There are those
who move
from here
to there,
who do
not walk,
but use
a chair."

"There are some
who read
in dark
of night,
by fingers
that
do not
need light."

"There are those
who sing
within
their hearts,
who cannot
hear
the flats
or sharps."

21

"For even those
who cannot walk,

or cannot hear
the words we talk,

or cannot see a
deep blue sky,

are nothing less
than you and I."

23

"They, too, have dreams they wish to keep. Their minds still dance though senses sleep."

The boy who
could walk
would never
again,
not ever
forget
the needs
of his
friend.

For the girl
in the seat
gave meaning
to strong.
She showed
there are
many
ways to
belong.

About the Author.....
Barry Rudner was born in Detroit, Michigan where he can still
be found to be growing up.

About the Illustrator.....
Peggy Trabalka, a wife of one and mother of three lovely
daughters, is a free-lance artist living in historic Milford,
Michigan. She has never seen a color she hasn't loved.

About the Publisher.....
Art-Print & Publishing Company (Tiny Thought Press) would like
to hear from you. Please call us at 1-800-456-3208 and tell us
what you think about *"The Handstand."* We are committed to
the enjoyment of children, parents and grandparents alike.

Other Tiny Thoughts at Local Stores . . .

The Littlest Tall Fellow

The Bumblebee and The Ram

Nonsense

Other Tiny Thoughts Coming Soon . . .

The Wind and The Skyscraper

The Statue and The Gift

The Nightmare

The Sound of One Hand Clapping

The Ring

Will I Still Have to Make My Bed in the Morning?

Plus others . . . .